FOUNDA__

ENEMIES IN THE LAND

An extract from 'Philippians'

JOHN METCALFE

Printed and Published by
John Metcalfe Publishing Trust
Church Road, Tylers Green
Penn, Buckinghamshire

Distributed by Trust Representatives
and Agents world-wide

In the Far East

Bethany, Orchard Point P.O. Box 0373
Singapore 9123

First Published May 1995

ISBN 1 870039 64 5

Price 25p

ENEMIES IN THE LAND

An Extract from 'Philippians'

'Be ye followers together of me', Phil. 3:17

IN Philippians Chapter 2 verses 12 to 16 Paul exhorts those whom he terms—and terms from the heart—'my beloved', that they should continue in obedience to work out their own salvation with fear and trembling, because it is God that worketh in them to will and to do of his good pleasure. That is, the very same volitions and earnest intentions which they themselves feel as Paul's obedient spiritual children, really have their origins from the hidden inworking of Almighty God.

However this exhortation, verse 12, commences with the word 'Wherefore', implying that a premise had been laid down on the basis of which this exhortation to outwork salvation follows. As if to say, This doctrine is true 'Wherefore', that exhortation follows.

Which doctrine is true? What premise follows? Why, the doctrine that a certain mind was in Christ Jesus. Notwithstanding that he was in the form of God, that he thought it not robbery to be equal with God, yet this mentality of unique humility and peerless self-sacrifice was in him. This took him down into death, yea, into the lower parts of the earth, in the meekest submission to the will of God.

So pleasing was this for God to behold in his beloved Son, that, raising him from the dead, bursting asunder the gates of death, sweeping aside the power of the grave, carrying him above all heavens, God highly exalted him. God has exalted him beyond all comprehension, so that not only is he Lord of all, but every knee shall be made to bow in submission, and every tongue shall be made to confess in subjection, whether friend or foe, devil or angel, sheep or goat.

In that great day of righteous recompence and just vengeance, every creature shall bow and confess the Lord of glory, before being sent to their place for eternity. Mark that, it is certain to come: every single creature, no matter their destiny, shall bow the knee and confess with the tongue the majesty, honour, and power of the Lord Jesus Christ on the throne of his glory.

Now, so to follow Christ in his humiliation; so to be as he was in the world; so to walk as we have him for an example; so to let this mind be in us which was in Christ Jesus; more: so to bow the knee continually in this present world and on earth; so to confess him before men throughout our remaining lifetime; that is, to do voluntarily throughout this present life, what all must do perforce at the end of it, this is to outwork salvation with a witness.

'Let this mind be in you, which was in Christ Jesus.' Here is no 'law as a rule of life'. No law ever given could have justly demanded or remotely required the depth of this humility. This is Christ as our life. 'Wherefore' what was true of his mentality, his mind, is to be outworked by the inworking of God, in all the brethren: 'For we have the mind of Christ.'

Whence it is to be observed that the whole doctrinal premise—'Wherefore'—of this remarkable and distinguished exhortation of the apostle Paul to the saints at Philippi lies in the truth of what Christ did for God, and for what in consequence God has done for Christ. That is the rule of life: to be fulfilled in our life and mentality with the lowliness of mind characteristic of every step in the life of the Redeemer.

'God hath highly exalted him', verse 9. Now, *that* is the resurrection, after such a sevenfold stoop, such a humiliating pathway, such a descent into death, on the part of the Saviour and on the behalf of his people. I say, *that* is the resurrection in Christ, the resurrection of the just, the resurrection to everlasting glory, to an eternal inheritance, the resurrection to the world to come whereof we speak.

There are things not to be missed in this remarkable exhortation, noticeable by their absence from contemporary Christendom. For example, the apostolic authority and the saints' submission.

First, the apostolic authority. The apostle was sent 'for *obedience* to the faith among all nations, for his name', Rom. 1:5, and again Rom. 15:18, 'to *make* the Gentiles *obedient*, by word and deed', hence, Rom. 6:17, 'Ye have *obeyed* from the heart that form of doctrine which was delivered you'. And, of course, in this place, Phil. 2:12, 'Wherefore, my beloved, as *ye have always obeyed*, not as in my presence only, but now much more in my absence.'

The apostles spake not their own word, did not their own will, died daily, lived by the faith of the Son of God, preached not themselves but Christ Jesus as Lord, Christ himself being mighty in them by the power of the Holy Ghost. And if these things be so of the apostolate, and of that holy ministry subject to the apostles, whose calling was confirmed by their word, then, Who among us today would not wish to be obedient, that is, much more in the apostles' absence, since their word alone provides us with the only inviolate, infallible, and certain direction in salvation?

Neither are these things obsolete, as though they passed away with the apostolic age. Otherwise where would we be, but utterly forsaken of God, and given up before we had so much as drawn breath? But 'Lo, I am with you alway, even unto the end of the age', Mt. 28:20, and again, Heb. 13:8 'Jesus Christ the same yesterday, and today, and for ever.' Then, as unchanging as is the Lord, so also are his ways. These things are not made obsolete with the passing of the apostles: though they honour and require subjection to those apostles.

Thus both the apostolic authority and the saints' submission are the same yesterday, today, and for ever, preserved in that apostolic ministry sent from the Son of God in heaven till the end of the age, and maintained in the saints gathered under that ministry and subject to its authority till the end of time.

Hence the apostle's association of Timothy with him in the joint authorship ascribed to the epistle. Though the writer was the apostle, and the disciple his son in the gospel, yet they are portrayed as one: 'Paul and Timotheus', Phil. 1:1.

This principle is even more apparent in the pastoral epistles, namely, I and II Timothy and Titus. From distant countries Paul directs the ministry in the absence of the apostleship, vesting in the sent and subject ministry of such as Timothy and Titus the authority—the sole authority—not only to continue and preserve the apostolic doctrine, fellowship, discipline, and ordinances, but to ordain elders, bishops, deacons. Moreover to mark out those called in their turn and place to the same work.

In the pastoral epistles the things to which the ministry sent from Christ must be strictly submissive are carefully written down. This serves two purposes: there can be no doubt of the duty of called ministers, and there can be no question of what the saints should—and must—expect from them. This known, written, and recorded duty cuts off the opportunity of false teachers remaining undetected, and it preserves the brethren of later ages—even to our own—from having the least possibility of being deceived. But what has happened? Generally, these particular pastoral apostolic writings have been either wrested, or treated with indifferent contempt.

This indisputable fact exposes the defiance of Plymouth Brethren teaching, which denies Christ's rights in both the ordination and the office of minister in its first principle. This system is guilty of overturning the scriptures written for the very purpose which it denies, particularly I and II Timothy and Titus. It terminates the apostolic ministry immediately after the death of the apostles and those appointed by them, reducing Timothy and Titus to the invented term 'delegates'.

Nothing could be more destructive of Christ's authority. However, the followers of J.N. Darby and the Plymouth Brethren justify this destructive razing of Zion's foundations by pointing to the errors of denominationalism and clerisy. Concerning what was wrong they may very well have been right: but—bolstered by their censorious correctness in judging the faults of others—what is this that they have substituted in the place of what they have ruined?

What? In the place of ruin they have put anarchy. The ruin of what? Of the continuity of Christ in sending the apostolic ministry, and of the requirement of that ministry to be faithful to Christ and his apostles by subject obedience and enforcement of the doctrine, discipline, and ordinance, laid down till the end of time in the epistles I and II Timothy and Titus.

So how dare these Brethren appoint themselves elders? According to the apostle only ordained ministers can appoint elders. However, denying the scripture its authority, and Christ his rights, they appoint themselves instead. Thus they cast out the ministry properly so-called, and put themselves in the seat they have just overthrown. Hence they rob the pastoral epistles of any force by denying the continuation of the office of those persons to whom alone what they usurp belongs.

Oh, yes, and they fill to overflowing the void they have thus made in scripture with the corruption of an ordinance not even mentioned in any one—much less in all three—of the pastoral epistles in question, putting *that*—as the papists put the Mass—instead of the central place of the preaching and teaching of the gospel by those sent to do so! Thus they destroy by a form the real means by which the saints are gathered and brought into divine unity, so to witness and function as one body according to the scriptures.

But the word of the Lord stands sure: 'How shall one preach except he be sent?' Sent? In place of Sending, Brethrenism substitutes Ruin, a system unscriptural, unevangelical, and anarchistic in its basic principle. This is at the root of Brethrenism. And neither the errors of Clericalism, nor the cherished mantra of the Brethren chanted against 'one-man ministry'—though charming never so wisely—can ever justify their heretical theory of Ruin by which they jettison the office of Minister and the scriptures written to govern that ministry.

Nor can it ever excuse this anarchistic and levelling system from its failure to return precisely to that order which was in the beginning. That is, to the apostolic authority on the one hand continued in the same subject ministry as Timothy and Titus; and to the saints' submission to that ministry on the other hand, both being sustained in the like humility. They will complain, 'But you cannot rebuild!' I answer, No: *but Christ can*. Only, your system disbelieves and prevents it by its avowed basis.

In contrast, how lovely it is to behold that order envisaged in Paul's beloved brethren, exhorted to lowly obedience, to do all things without murmurings and disputings, blameless and harmless, the sons of God without rebuke. And this amidst a crooked and perverse nation, a hostile world, a scene of adversity. But it is God that worketh in—that is, within—the saints, and, together, they are to work out their own salvation with fear and trembling.

How such trembling reverence has departed from the present generation. The fear of God is today conspicuous by its absence. Yet of the first saints it was written 'Great fear came upon all the church'. They feared, yes, and trembled. But where has all this gone? It has gone with the departure of the glory. It has long gone; and the people are hardened. Ichabod is over the whole generation: 'For the glory is departed.'

At the beginning, in the very atmosphere of eternity, with the felt presence of the living God, the saints trembled together under the mighty power of the salvation of God:

it is not, 'Work out *thine* own salvation'. It is 'Work out *your* own salvation'.

Here was one people, in the fear of God, separated from the world, indwelt by Father, Son, and Holy Ghost, outworking salvation in one body, so that, holding forth the word of life, they shone as lights in the darkness of this world. Enduring to the end. So the apostle would rejoice in the day of Christ, that he had not run in vain, neither laboured in vain:

'Beloved, as ye always have
  obeyed me heretofore,
not only when I present am,
  but in my absence more,

Work ye your own salvation out,
  as is both meet and due,
with fear and trembling evident
  in every one of you.

Because that it is God which doth
  work in you inwardly,
that thereby of his pleasure good
  both will and do might ye.

Do all things without murmurings,
  disputings, or discord:
that wholly blameless ye may be,
  the harmless sons of God;

Those 'gainst whom there is no rebuke,
  although ye should be found
amidst a crooked nation where
  perverseness doth abound;

Among whom also in the world
as lights ye shine abroad,
as one together holding forth
of life the very word.'

Next Paul declares his readiness to be 'offered up', as if on an altar. That is, since his imprisonment and trial were from no cause other than persecution for his preaching the gospel, it would be upon the altar of that preaching having been made effectual to the Gentiles that he would be offered: a willing and thankful victim 'Offered upon the sacrifice and service of your faith'.

Since that faith came to them by the pure, only, and true gospel of the grace of Christ preached by Paul, he adds the explanation: 'If', he writes, he should be sacrificed on such an altar, 'I joy, and rejoice with you all'. Then let them not mourn, but joy and rejoice with him.

They were not to despair as though all were lost: all was gained. There was nothing in this life but Christ, whom they had gained by the very gospel which provided the occasion for Paul's sacrifice. And, as to that sacrifice, 'to die is gain'.

Following this, Paul speaks of his purposing to send Timotheus, but not before he knew how it would go with him at the trial. As to Timothy, as a son with the father he had served with Paul in the gospel, and this had been proven over long years of experience.

There was no other minister left to Paul of like mind. Phil. 2:20, 'For I have no man likeminded, who will naturally care for your state.' And if that were true *then*, what can one expect *now*? I expect Christ in his great faithfulness still to send if it be but one or two likeminded sons to the apostle, till the last day; sons, that is, who will, on the one hand, 'naturally care for your state', and, on the other, willingly be 'offered up upon the sacrifice and service of your faith'.

Now appears a most revealing statement, Phil. 2:21, 'For all seek their own, not the things which are Jesus Christ's.' Do remember the era in which this was written: that is, during the lifetime of the apostles. And, realizing, ask yourself whether you think to escape controversy, affliction, declension, apathy, division, complacency, apostasy, a great falling away, a famine of the word of God, an absence of sent ministers, yes, and persecution, enmity, adversity, suffering, trial, and even death, in such a latter day as this?

Ask yourself what does this expression mean 'All seek their own', an expression that must in the nature of things be vastly compounded as time passes, so that beyond measure today, 'All seek their own, not the things which are Jesus Christ's'?

And mark this: it was not that they did not *profess* Jesus Christ. It was that *whilst* professing him, they couldn't care less about his things, because they were entirely occupied with their own: 'All seek their own.'

This is to be a foolish builder; a goat and not a sheep. This is to be seed sown on bad ground. This is to be a foolish virgin. This is to lay up for oneself the words at the last judgment: 'Depart from me: I never knew you.'

But then, what *are* the things of Jesus Christ which no man in those countries save Paul and Timotheus sought in the ministry, since 'all'— *all*—'seek their own', using *his* things as a means of gaining *theirs*? Yes, but, precisely what constitutes 'the things which are Jesus Christ's'?

Well, for example: The old testament. It is his: it is only lent to us. The new testament. It is not our property, or scholars' property: it is one of his things. The holy bible.

The Greek text owned of him from the beginning, and, in principle, recovered at the Reformation, called The *Textus Receptus*. Likewise the English translation owned of God for centuries: the Authorized Version, largely taken from the martyr Tyndale's much earlier translation, bought for us today at the price of his being strangled and burned at the stake.

The entire gospel, in every part, and the sum of the parts: all this—every part of it—is Jesus Christ's, and no one else's. No thief has the right to subtract from it; no ripper to lacerate it; no heretic to divide it; no Arminian to multiply it; no legalist to add to it: it is *his*. And his *as it is*.

This evangel declares his Person, his one Person, his divine Person; his Sonship, his eternal Sonship; his incarnation, his humanity; his having both divine and human natures in union without confusion in one Person; his body, his blood; his perfection, his spirituality; his immensity, his humility: in a word, the mystery that is Christ. It is his: his to reveal, his to obscure; his to give, his to withhold. Sovereignly, imperatively, absolutely, in his own prerogative, all is his.

His life is his: from eternity; throughout the old testament; within the new testament; in glory; to eternity. The work of Christ is his: his birth; his baptism; his transfiguration; his visitation; his death; his resurrection; his ascension. His ministry is his: his Galilean ministry; his ministry on the way; his Jerusalem ministry; his ministry from the glory.

His divine administration is his: the ministration of justification; of life; of reconciliation; of the word; of the Spirit; of the new testament; and of the glory. All these things are his, his to give, his to withhold. None can claim them: he can bestow them. But they are his absolutely. No one has a *right* to what is his.

The ministry is his: whether of the Spirit in the body, which is one thing; or whether from the Head to the body, which is another thing. These things are Christ's. They do not belong to colleges, or principals, or tutors. They are *his*. And his to send directly to the people, fully prepared, from the heavenly glory, and by the indwelling Spirit.

The church—the *ecclesia*—is his. It is not man's: it is not for man to take over, divide, reorganize, or copy in various denominations as though each separate division were the church. It is not for man to manage, appoint, elect, or set up in rivalry the one division against the other—indeed there is no justification for the existence of *any* other than *his own* church.

Those churches that are of man; or those sects, denominations or apostasies which they invent; or halls, societies, or congregations which they set up: all of them, not being *his*, should be shut down immediately. It is a fearful compound of robbery, presumption, and arrogance. The nature, administration, and gathering of the church should be left in faith to him whose right it is to be the one Head of one body. After all, what would *you* think if you came out of anaesthetic with a dozen more heads from other men grafted on as many dismembered parts of other creatures onto *your* divided body?

The ordinances are his, and his to ordain. It is not for the Queen, or for the Prime Minister, or for some advisory body, much less for foreigners from Rome, nor yet the church membership, neither the Brethren hall, to ordain bishops, or elect deacons, or raise up elders: this is *his* sole right, and he alone can perform it. Order is his. Prayer is his. Baptism is his. The Supper is his.

The psalms are his; the spiritual songs are his; the hymns of the new testament are his; all being called 'The word of Christ' in song. These things are not ours, either for poets or would-be hymn writers to invent, they are his to convey. Nor ought we to sing *anything* but what he bestows and commands.

Likewise with worship. It is his: he must lead it, and lead it by his own Spirit. Worship is in Spirit and truth; it is in sonship; it is to the Father; and Christ leads it: these are his things. There is no place for man here; no place for the flesh. God cannot away with what is of man or the flesh. Only what is of Christ is acceptable with God. Time fails to tell of Christ's things! The inheritance is his, the hope, the resurrection, the glory, and the world to come. All things are Christ's.

I confess to you, I love, love, love these things. His things. I love them, and love every one of them, and I love him, so much, I cannot hold my peace: let them cast me out if they will. God knoweth, my conscience bears me witness, I live for his things, I cannot tolerate man taking over any one of them: no, not the least of them. I live for them, and by grace, by my God, I would die for them.

These are the things which are Jesus Christ's; which in Paul's day, no man sought after, 'For all seek their own, not the things which are Jesus Christ's.' And do you think, in the very nature of things, it is any better now? Or does not your own conscience tell you, Rather, it is far worse now?

So Paul purposes to send Timothy, his own son in the gospel, who sought the things which are Jesus Christ's, and lived for them, likeminded with Paul. But before that he would send Epaphroditus, their messenger, and his brother and companion, who risked his life to fulfil their service and sacrifice to Paul. Now the apostle, in turn, hastens to restore this faithful servant of Christ to the Philippians.

Thus Paul comes to Philippians Chapter 3, evidently intending to conclude the epistle at this point, Phil. 3:1, 'Finally, my brethren'. But it is far from finally, and thankful all saints should be for the long digression—a kind of parenthesis—because in fact it is not until into Chapter 4 that the apostle returns to his originally intended conclusion, repeating the words 'Finally, brethren', Phil. 4:8. But what made him digress?

He had said, Phil. 3:1, 'Finally, my brethren, rejoice in the Lord.' Did he digress to expound on the subject of rejoicing? No, not upon that. But so often he exhorted to joy and rejoicing, it was indeed a repetition, hence he says 'to write the same'—for he knows he is repeating himself—'to write the same things to me indeed is not grievous.' This is no more than an explanation of his repeated exhortation to rejoice.

Then what makes him digress after 'finally' in 3:1, throughout Chapter 3, continuing beyond into the first seven verses of Chapter 4, before returning to the words, 'Finally, brethren', Phil. 4:8?

What? It is a digression springing entirely from the last, closing, phrase in 3:1, 'For you it is safe'. It was their *safety*. *That* moved his heart, stirred his bowels, flashed with divine light in his mind: their *safety*. Now, safety is *salvation*. It is at this point that the extended digression occurs.

Safety is from *danger*. Salvation is out of the hand of *enemies*. But fools make a mock of danger. The simple trust enemies. Here, Paul would have them to be wise: to know their enemies: to be *safe*. Hence he proceeds to warn them immediately, Ch. 3:2.

'*Beware*'. There can be no word more closely associated with *the warning of what is unsafe*. For their safety, therefore, the apostle proceeds to describe exactly of whom to beware. Said the Lord Jesus 'Beware of men'. Saith Paul, 'Beware of dogs, beware of evil workers, beware of the concision', Phil. 3:2. You see how plainly Paul speaks, and under what strong characterization he describes the enemies of the saints and of the gospel, without deliverance from whom they could not be saved.

And are we so safe today, that it is all right that we are kept even from hearing such plainness of speech, and denied on every hand such clearness of warning? No, we are not so safe: we are in more danger today, than were the Philippians in their day. Then why does nobody warn us with equal, if not more vehement, force?

Why? Because the enemies of whom Paul warned the Philippians have now filled the churches, denominations, and halls, so as to control them, and hence they are hardly likely to warn us against themselves. And if it be not so, Why do we hear no warnings?

For Paul warns of dogs, evil workers, and the concision, *in* the church, not out of it. In the then undivided church, not the present divided and denominated one. If so, *how much more* ought we to be warned for our safety, and, at that, without any mealy-mouthed mumbling, mincing of words, or beating about the bush? But platitudes and affected 'niceness' are all that we get, leaving us without a clue either of the danger, the urgency, the antidote, or the way of safety.

But we trust in God, that you may find us without dissimulation, and faithful followers of Paul in the holy word of God, subject to the immense authority of the apostles, and caring for your priceless safety. Thus we shall speak to you the word of truth, the gospel of your salvation, with all boldness, come what may. Hence we proceed to show you not only the meaning of the apostle, and those of whom he warns the Philippians, but the meaning to us, and of whom he cautions us also.

First the apostle warns us of dogs. But what does he mean by 'dogs'? One of three things: either literal dogs; or those worldly men who so act like dogs that he calls them by that name; or else religious dogs of the same nature in the church. Since the threefold warning goes on to speak of what undoubtedly refers to religious men, we may safely conclude that he bids us beware of religious dogs.

Well, from the contemporary dissolution of all plain speaking into characterless sentiment, you would think that Paul's 'dogs' are an ancient canine species which became quite extinct no sooner than described. Is that so? Let us see.

The twenty-second Psalm is famous for its prophetic vision and pin-point accuracy over the events of the crucifixion of

Christ some nine hundred years before Jesus either came into the world, or was, at the last, nailed to the cross. 'They part my garments among them, and cast lots upon my vesture', cried David in a prophetic trance.

Nearly a whole millennium later John the apostle, who saw the crucifixion from beginning to end—and you know that his witness is true—told of this very event, which took place before his eyes, 'They parted my raiment among them, and for my vesture they cast lots. These things therefore the soldiers did', John 19:24.

David saw in vision centuries beforehand that which made him cry out—not knowing what he said, nor why he said it—being full of the Holy Ghost, 'They pierced my hands and my feet'! But they did not. No one pierced David's hands and feet. But, saith Peter on the Day of Pentecost, 'David, being a prophet', 'seeing this before', 'spake of Christ.'

Nine hundred years after David spake of Christ, Christ came. But they hung the Saviour on a tree, in the process of which they nailed him through his hands and his feet. This was called Crucifixion, in which, even as David foresaw, they pierced Christ's hands and feet.

And as if this were not testimony enough, Jesus, risen from the dead, rebukes to this day the blind unbelief of man in Thomas, who had said, 'Except I shall see in his hands the print of the nails, and put my finger into the print of the nails, and thrust my hand into his side, I will not believe.' Came Jesus, risen from the dead, and said,

'Reach hither thy finger, and behold my hands; and reach hither thy hand, and thrust it into my side: and be not faithless, but believing', Jn. 20:27.

'Be not faithless'? Why faithless? Because of unbelief: 'O fools, and slow of heart to believe all that the prophets have spoken.' Near a thousand years before it happened, David prophetically described in detail *exactly* what was to take place a thousand years later. And yet, is even *that* any more remarkable than the demonstrable proof shown to Thomas by Jesus after he had risen from the dead?

Case after case might be multiplied from Psalm 22 of what would be absolutely incredible except for two things: First, the omniscience of God, by whom David saw forward into the yawning future, prophesying what would happen nine hundred years before each detail unfolded moment by moment when the time was fulfilled. Second, the unshakeable reliability of the scriptures: 'O fools' said Jesus, 'and slow of heart to believe *all* that the prophets have spoken.' This rebuke was delivered to the disciples after Jesus was risen from the dead, with the marks verifying that death plain for all to see.

But what is all this to do with dogs? Psalm 22:16 states 'For dogs have compassed me: the assembly of the wicked have inclosed me: they pierced my hands and my feet.' But who compassed Jesus? Judas, one of the twelve. He led the assembly of the wicked which compassed Jesus about at Gethsemane. He led them to the palace of the high priest. Unlawfully Jesus was condemned by the chief priests. They haled him into their assembly. That assembly was called, The Sanhedrin.

The Sanhedrin was composed of the chief priests, elders, scribes, Pharisees, Sadducees, doctors, rulers of the people, with the whole hierarchy of the religious system. This was the assembly which compassed him about. None other.

True, they outmanoeuvred and trapped Pilate into commanding the soldiers actually to do the work of piercing Jesus' hands and feet. You say, Then it was Pilate. Or the soldiers. Peter the apostle says, 'Ye men of Israel, hear these words; Jesus of Nazareth *ye* have taken, and by wicked hands have crucified and slain', Acts 2:22,23.

Now, find the modern equivalent of the chief priests, elders, rulers of the people, the scribes, the Pharisees, the Sadducees, the doctors, the Herodians, the entire hierarchy of religious leaders, and you have found Peter's 'Ye', David's 'Assembly', and Paul's 'Dogs'.

If not, what *does* it mean, since—despite modern incredulity—this breed is not said to have become extinct, but rather to have increased so much the more till at the last they have filled and taken over the professing church, or, as scripture calls it, the 'outer court'. Beware of dogs.

Next Paul warns the brethren of 'evil workers'. These are the same as those elsewhere called 'workers of iniquity', and, of course, refers to the religious of this sort, not the worldly.

Do bear in mind the context, in which Paul intended to conclude this epistle 'finally', 3:1, by exhorting his brethren to rejoice in the Lord. This exhortation, however repetitive, was safe. That word, 'Safe', triggered the parenthetical digression with which we are now concerned. Safe? Then in the following verses he interrupts his once 'final' conclusion: Safety lies in the avoidance of dogs, evil workers, and the concision.

As we see here, at the centre of this dangerous triad lies those whom Paul calls 'evil workers' or 'workers of iniquity'. We know that they infiltrate and permeate the church—the *ecclesia*—we know that they are religious, but the question remains, What gives them their distinctive character among the three the avoidance of each of whom is essential to escape from deadly and everlasting danger?

Evil workers are those who do not, and will not, follow the apostolic ministry, and, to put it plainly, the apostolic minister, either in Paul himself, or in his son Timothy, or in those subsequently sent from the Head, Christ, in the heavenly glory. The ministers they defy are those who manifest their meek subjection and submission to Christ and his apostles in their doctrine, discipline, fellowship, ordinances, and authoritative insistence and enforcement of the same, to the end of the age.

Whoso claims apostolic authority, or ministry, or pastoral office, or gift, or place, yet fails to follow those in whom this example is manifest, there you find the evil worker. 'Brethren, be followers together of me, and *mark them* which walk, *so as ye have us*—plural: *us—for an ensample*', Phil. 3:17.

And how do you walk, Paul, Timothy, and those who follow your example, whom the brethren are to follow to this day, marking *your* walk in contrast to that of those evil workers who refuse to walk in your exemplary way, or to tread in your footsteps? 'For many walk, of whom I have told you often'—so that you see the apostle *never avoided the naming of persons or parties dangerous to the safety of the brethren, or of the church, no matter what controversy or hatred this stirred up against himself*—'many walk of whom I have told you often, and now tell you even weeping.'

Weeping, not for *them*, the evil workers, but for the havoc which they would work in God's assembly, the divisions they would cause in the one *ecclesia*, the church, and the multitudes who, blinded by their trickery, would increasingly wander out of the way of understanding, into the depth of destruction, by following these evil workers, elsewhere called 'blind leaders of the blind', whose end is to fall into the ditch of everlasting darkness.

What marked them out? Nothing too obvious. That is, unless one laid the apostolic walk against their walk, and the apostolic word against their word, and the apostles' fellowship against their fellowship, which soon showed how cross their path was to that of the apostolic ministry.

What was the evil of these 'evil workers'? Nothing too obvious. That is, unless one marked the righteousness which characterized the apostolic ministry, which soon made apparent the unrighteousness of these evil workers, who, under the guise of 'love' dissolved all righteousness into a liquid morass of adaptability to the flesh, the world, and an outward show of Christianity.

What marked out these evil workers? First, They are 'the enemies of the cross of Christ', Phil. 3:18. How was that? Because they did not preach the substitutionary atonement, namely, that Christ actually redeemed his people when he died; that of necessity he died for the sheep and not for the goats; and that he really and effectually purchased his people with his own blood when it was shed.

Hence, by his blood, at the cross, Christ brought in a divine righteousness which was reckoned or imputed to the account of his elect *then*, a righteousness exterior to themselves, in the bank of heaven, credited to their account *at the moment at which Christ died*, a righteousness which is said to be 'unto them'—Rom. 3:22—through the death of Christ. This righteousness is at the very heart of the gospel. To it sinners and the ungodly are called. When these believe, then that which was before 'unto them', is, at the moment of believing, 'upon them', Rom. 3:22.

God thus imputes righteousness, in their conscious knowledge of it, so that their faith now credits—in their own experience—what the blood of Christ *had* obtained for them, and what God *had* laid up for them, at the time at which Christ died. Now, however, *they* are aware of it, God conveys the knowledge of it to their own belief, and when he does this, believers are said to be justified by faith. This is a most wholesome doctrine, and very full of comfort.

But evil workers are the enemies of this doctrine. They hate it. Then, they are the enemies of the cross of Christ. They walk contrary to it. But Paul walked by it, and to this day calls you to follow his example by us who follow him, and mark those who walk contrary thereto, so as to beware of them.

Well, try out this rule for yourselves, for we can do nothing against the truth, but only for it. Therefore we have declared to you plainly that they are enemies of the cross of Christ who do not distinctly, clearly, and continuously preach and walk by this doctrine, though such deviates fill the pulpits, halls, and churches the length and breadth of Great Britain.

And of this truth our own Articles tell us, namely, 'That we are justified by faith only is a most wholesome doctrine, and very full of comfort', Article XI of the Thirty-nine Articles of the Church of England. This Article on Justification is true. But justification rests on atonement. And atonement was wrought for all the elect at the cross of Christ.

Whoso preaches otherwise, or walks otherwise, or fails to preach this continually, Paul designates an 'evil worker', because they are 'enemies of the cross of Christ'. Hence the apostle warns you to avoid such, as you would avoid an injection of anthrax, AIDS, and the bubonic plague all mixed up in the same syringe, about to be plunged into your life-blood.

'Whose end is destruction', Phil. 3:19. So was the end of those who contracted the black death. But the black death of those who follow the false teachers whom Paul designates as the enemies of the cross of Christ—who profess by beguiling words to hold the very thing of which they are enemies, though they never preach or walk by it as did Paul—I say, the black death of those who follow these deceivers is that of outer darkness and a bottomless pit. 'Whose end is destruction.'

They sentimentalize the crucifixion: but they rubbish justification. They depict Jesus on the cross: yet they vandalize substitutionary atonement. They can coo, croon, or rock their choruses, but they cannot teach, reason, or instruct on ransom, reconciliation, propitiation, expiation, oblation, redemption, remission, nor are the words substitutionary atonement in their mouths, and as to their hearts, with all their strength they detest and hate imputed righteousness and justification by faith only.

'Whose end is destruction', and, it follows, since they are blind leaders of the blind, all who follow them shall fall into the like ditch. But follow Paul. Follow the apostolic ministry. Follow Article XI. 'Be ye followers together of me', says the apostle. Well: there is his example, in both doctrine and walk, and what could be more plain, more illuminating, or more honestly set before you?

Paul comes to the next characteristic of these deadly invaders of the church: 'Whose God is their belly.' Now do not be deceived by the apparent simplicity of this statement. Not literally their belly. Not merely that they are gluttons. For, here, *the belly is envisaged as the seat of the appetites.*

Which appetites? Oh, any appetites. Such as greed; ambition; place-seeking; flattery; pride; snobbery; lust; uncleanness; enmity; hatred; emulation; strife; vain glory; covetousness: the 'belly' holds them all. And these enemies of the cross of Christ so pursued their appetites; so connived at lust to fulfil them; so lived for them, so winked at the same thing in others; that the life and vigour they put into *that* was precisely the life and vigour they *should* have put into *worship*.

Then, that *was* their worship. If so, their god was the self-gratification of those appetites. As saith the apostle Paul of these evil workers, the enemies of the cross of Christ, Phil. 3:19, 'whose God is their belly'.

Then, 'their glory is in their shame', Phil. 3:19. They glory in appearances, II Cor. 5:12; they glory in condemnation, II Cor. 3:9; they glory in men, I Thess. 2:6; they glory in vanity, Gal. 5:26; they glory in man's praise, Mt. 6:2; they glory in the flesh, Gal. 6:13: but they do not glory in the Lord, I Cor. 1:31, and hence they come short of the glory of God, Rom. 3:23, having their part with the hypocrites, the unjust, the unwise virgins, and the goats.

And what are these doing, these evil workers, whose glory is in their shame, not only taking part in, but actually taking over, the Christian ministry? 'Whose glory is in their shame'?

Finally, as opposed to the apostle, his son Timothy, and all those ministers sent of Christ to follow Paul's example from the beginning, whose conversation was and is in heaven, from whence they looked and look for the Saviour, the Lord Jesus Christ, these 'evil workers', in total contrast, 'mind earthly things', Phil. 3:19.

But the apostle looked not on the things which can be seen, but on the things which cannot be seen, II Cor. 4:18. Those who followed the apostle, through his doctrine, were transformed by the renewing of their minds, Rom. 12:2, but the minds of those who followed the false teachers, who 'minded earthly things', never were transformed. They were worldly, conformed to this world, minding fleshly things, earthly things.

These earthly-minded false teachers sought the praise of man, their own advantage, and the whitewash of the hypocrite. They were carnally minded, were of the world, and the world heard them, and, after all, what else would one expect of evil workers, enemies of the cross of Christ, whose end is destruction, whose God is their belly, those whose mentality never rises above the flesh and this present world, who, in total contrast to the apostle and the apostolic ministry, 'minded earthly things', Phil. 3:19?

But one more example will suffice to show the nature and the deceit of those the avoidance of whom Paul declares to be a criterion of our safety. These 'evil workers', or, as Jesus names them, 'workers of iniquity', are described in the famous Sermon on the Mount, as it is said, 'Many will say to me in that day, Lord, Lord, have we not prophesied in thy name? and in thy name have cast out devils? and in thy name done many wonderful works?' Mt. 7:22.

Here you see that they lack not claim to miracles, who iniquitously rebel against the apostle, his doctrine, and the example of the apostolic ministry. They cover up their rebellion by claiming the signs of an apostle, whilst at the same time they revolt against the true apostolic authority.

But what miracle do we read of in Timothy? What miracle was ever wrought by Titus, Epaphras, Sylvanus, or any other whom the apostle counted as his sons in the ministry of the gospel? They were not apostles, but they were obedient to the apostles. Therefore they had no apostolic signs: what they had was apostolic obedience.

Hence, these evil workers pretend to signs and miracles, to disguise the fact that Christ had neither called them nor sent them, God had neither wrought in them nor spoken by them, and the Holy Ghost had neither verified their false doctrine nor anointed their corrupt preaching. Oh, but they would claim visions of the virgin; images of the saints; miracles in the grotto; and I know not what other fables, to beguile the simple.

And today, they will claim to prophesy in his name, speak tongues in gibberish, receive a spirit other than the Holy Spirit, heal the sick, change water into wine, or even raise the dead. And, if there be any other devilish blasphemy whereby they may say that God has done through them, for shame, no less than he did by Christ and his apostles, they will claim that also, finally to strut onto the stage at the last judgment with this brash familiarity: 'Lord, Lord!'

Then the truth will out: for they and their followers will hear the first, the last, and the only words Christ ever spoke to them in their whole lives, so to ring in their ears for the rest of eternity: 'I never knew you: depart from me, *ye that work iniquity*', Mt. 7:23.

And by this—that is, the claim to have performed apostolic miracles—no matter that deceitful and deceiving apostates of great evangelical repute have put their stamp on it, you may see that pentecostalism and the charismatic delusion are nothing but the deceit of evil workers. It is no different from the ancient Roman Catholic claimed sights and signs of the Madonna, or cures at Lourdes, or speaking in tongues at Avila, or preposterous fables concerning miracles from the relics of the saints.

Moreover you can see plainly that those who perpetrate and fabricate such absurd pretensions, whether ancient or modern, are nothing but what the apostle plainly calls 'evil workers', Phil. 3:2, on the one hand, and the Lord Jesus condemns as 'workers of iniquity', Mt. 7:23, on the other.

But there is a final group named by Paul to complete this unholy triad. They are called 'the concision', or, 'the mutilators'. The apostle employs a biting irony, a sarcasm that liberal evangelicals would not merely find distasteful, they would be moved to indignation—a rare performance—to say that it was positively unchristian, or 'unloving'. For by this cliché, as to the manner born, they reduce all character to a common absurdity.

But Almighty God and the Father; the Son of the living God, the Lord Jesus Christ; the Holy Ghost from heaven, the Spirit of truth, giving forth the sacred scripture of the new testament by the holy apostles, to whom its infallibility was entrusted, used the language 'Dogs; evil workers; the concision'. And who is he that will question that?

Why, the modern evangelical apostasy will question it. The love of God, of Christ, of the Spirit of truth, of the new testament, is not loving enough for them. But Paul with holy boldness sarcastically uses the parody 'concision' for 'circumcision' for two reasons.

First, circumcision never was an end in itself: it was a means to an end given to Abraham, of whom it is said 'He received the *sign* of circumcision', Rom. 4:11. But everybody knows the only value of a sign lies in the thing which it signifies.

And what did the sign of circumcision signify? That *the flesh had been taken away, cut off*, in the birth of Abraham's true seed. But the Jews were full of the flesh. Far from cutting off the flesh, they were nothing but flesh. Then their sign was worthless, nothing but a pointless mutilation.

Their sign was worthless: they were the concision: they mutilated themselves for nothing. 'If thou be a breaker of the law, thy circumcision is made uncircumcision.' 'For he is not a Jew, which is one outwardly; *neither is that circumcision, which is outward in the flesh*: But he is a Jew, which is one inwardly; *and circumcision is that of the heart*, in the spirit, and not in the letter; whose praise is not of men, but of God', Rom. 2:28,29.

Now these legalistic hypocrites gloried in creeping into the *ecclesia*, demanding the Gentile believers to be under the law as a rule of life, and, to verify their subjection thereto, to submit to circumcision. But Paul says, it is *not* circumcision: it is concision, and they who do it are mutilators. Antinomian, unevangelical, legalistic mutilators. And so are their Presbyterian, Westminsterite, imitators who follow their false teaching but deftly dispense with its sign.

Not only did these hypocrites, these whited sepulchres, fail to keep the law themselves, but they turned it into an outward show of forms and ceremonies, mutilating its true nature, thus making themselves wholly offensive to God. They themselves never understood the circumcision which they demanded of the Gentiles. For, if it signified not being born after the flesh, it pointed to being born of God.

But these understood neither sign nor pointer, both of which were fulfilled in the gospel of Christ. For Christ in the cross *had* taken away the flesh, not in a sign but in the reality, and, justified in him, *that true circumcision* was fulfilled already in the Gentiles, who had been born of God: 'For we are the'—true, inward—'circumcision, which worship God in the spirit, and rejoice in Christ Jesus, and have no confidence in the flesh', Phil. 3:3.

But this 'concision', these 'mutilators', insinuated themselves into the church in Paul's absence, saying that 'The gospel was all very well, but you must keep the law'—that is, their whitewashed hypocritical outward form of it—'as a rule of life *as well*; and, as a sign of this, you must be circumcised.' Vile mutilators! Vile mutilators of law, of the gospel, of the sign, and of the thing signified. 'For Christ is the end of the law for righteousness to every one that believeth', Rom. 10:4, and 'In him also ye *are* circumcised with the circumcision made without hands', Col. 2:11.

What need then of mutilators? 'For we are the circumcision, which worship God in the spirit, and rejoice in Christ Jesus, and have no confidence in the flesh', Phil. 3:3. Then whether with the sign or without the sign; whether requiring circumcision or not requiring circumcision: Beware of dogs; beware of evil workers; beware of the concision, who would undo all that Christ has already accomplished for us in the cross, circumcision and all, besides totally delivering us from the law as such, whether under such euphemisms as 'a rule of life', or not: totally delivering us, 'that we might live unto God'.

Beware, I say, sign or not, beware as you would dread the very plague, beware of those who claim by the traditions of men—but contrary to the XIth of the Thirty-nine Articles —I say, beware of those who claim that the law, whilst not a rule of justification, is nevertheless a rule of life. If you receive that, you have been mutilated in your soul. Christ is our life, and Christ is all.

'I through the law am dead to the law, that I might live unto God. I am crucified with Christ', Gal. 2:19,20. And, if so, we are circumcised in him not by the sign, but in the reality, when he for us 'put off the body of the sin of the flesh by the circumcision of Christ', Col. 2:11, that is, through being made sin in his vicarious sacrifice at the cross.

But to this day there are those—not in the outward form of circumcision, now outmoded as a sign of being under the law to work for life—nevertheless, I say, there are those who, dispensing with the sign, would still bring us under bondage by the substance. The Substance? Yes, that we should walk by the law as a rule of life. And, compared to *that* enormity, what is the sign? Nothing. But the substance is a matter of life and death.

They say, It is a matter of life. Paul declares, The law brings nothing but wrath; it only genders a curse; it cannot give life; it shuts up to bondage; and is altogether and wholly a sentence of death.

All these defiant enemies who say otherwise are mutilators of our souls; butchers of the gospel; and Antinomian *charcutiers* against the law. They are called, The Concision. To this day. Saith the apostle, Beware of them.

For, says the apostle in his holy doctrine, 'Christ is the end of the law for righteousness to every one that believeth', Rom. 10:4; and, 'I through the law am dead to the law, that I might live unto God', Gal 2:19. 'Wherefore, my brethren, ye also are become dead to the law by the body of

Christ; that ye should be married to another, even to him who is raised from the dead, that we should bring forth fruit unto God', Rom. 7:4.

So the apostle concludes, Rom. 7:6, 'But now we are delivered from the law, that being dead wherein we were held; that we should serve in newness of spirit, and not in the oldness of the letter.'

JOHN METCALFE

MINISTRY BY JOHN METCALFE

TAPE MINISTRY BY JOHN METCALFE
FROM ENGLAND AND THE FAR EAST
IS AVAILABLE.

In order to obtain this free recorded ministry, please send your blank cassette (C.90) and the cost of the return postage, including your name and address in block capitals, to the John Metcalfe Publishing Trust, Church Road, Tylers Green, Penn, Bucks, HP10 8LN. Tapelists are available on request.

Owing to the increased demand for the tape ministry, we are unable to supply more than two tapes per order, except in the case of meetings for the hearing of tapes, where a special arrangement can be made.

Book Order Form

Please send to the address below:-

		Price	Quantity
A Question for Pope John Paul II		£1.25	......
Of God or Man?		£1.45	......
Noah and the Flood		£1.90	......
Divine Footsteps		£0.95	......
The Red Heifer		£0.75	......
The Wells of Salvation		£1.50	......
The Book of Ruth (Hardback edition)		£4.95	......
Divine Meditations of William Huntington		£2.35	......
Present-Day Conversions of the New Testament Kind		£2.25	......
Saving Faith		£2.25	......
Deliverance from the Law		£1.90	......
The Beatitudes		£1.90	......
Colossians		£0.95	......
Philippians		£1.90	......
Matthew		£0.95	......
Philemon		£l.90	......
Psalms, Hymns & Spiritual Songs (Hardback edition)			
The Psalms of the Old Testament		£2.50	......
Spiritual Songs from the Gospels		£2.50	......
The Hymns of the New Testament		£2.50	......
'Apostolic Foundation of the Christian Church' series			
Foundations Uncovered	Vol.I	£0.75	......
The Birth of Jesus Christ	Vol.II	£0.95	......
The Messiah (Hardback)	Vol.III	£7.75	......
The Son of God and Seed of David (Hardback)	Vol.iV	£6.95	......
Christ Crucified (Hardback)	Vol.V	£6.95	......
Justification by Faith (Hardback)	Vol.VI	£7.50	......
The Church: What is it? (Hardback)	Vol.VII	£7.75	......

Name and Address (in block capitals)

. . . .

. . . .

. . . .

If money is sent with order please allow for postage. Please address to:- The John Metcalfe Publishing Trust, Church Road, Tylers Green, Penn, Bucks, HP10 8LN.

THE MINISTRY OF THE NEW TESTAMENT

The purpose of this substantial A4 gloss paper magazine is to provide spiritual and experimental ministry with sound doctrine which rightly and prophetically divides the Word of Truth.

Readers of our books will already know the high standards of our publications. They can be confident that these pages will maintain that quality, by giving access to enduring ministry from the past, much of which is derived from sources that are virtually unobtainable today, and publishing a living ministry from the present. Selected articles from the following writers have already been included:

ELI ASHDOWN · ABRAHAM BOOTH · JOHN BRADFORD
JOHN BUNYAN · JOHN BURGON · JOHN CALVIN · DONALD CARGILL
JOHN CENNICK · J.N. DARBY · GEORGE FOX · JOHN FOXE
WILLIAM GADSBY · JOHN GUTHRIE · WILLIAM GUTHRIE
GREY HAZLERIGG · WILLIAM HUNTINGTON · WILLIAM KELLY
JOHN KENNEDY · JOHN KERSHAW · HANSERD KNOLLYS
JAMES LEWIS · MARTIN LUTHER · ROBERT MURRAY MCCHEYNE
JOHN METCALFE · ALEXANDER—SANDY—PEDEN · J.C. PHILPOT
J.K. POPHAM · JAMES RENWICK · J.B. STONEY · HENRY TANNER
ARTHUR TRIGGS · JOHN VINALL · JOHN WARBURTON
JOHN WELWOOD · GEORGE WHITEFIELD · J.A. WYLIE

Magazine Order Form

Name and Address (in block capitals)

. . . .

. . . .

. . . .

Please send me .... current copy/copies of The Ministry of the New Testament.

Please send me .... year/s subscription.

I enclose a cheque/postal order for £ ....

(Price: including postage, U.K. £1.75; Overseas £1.90)
(One year's subscription: Including postage, U.K. £7.00; Overseas £7.60)

Cheques should be made payable to The John Metcalfe Publishing Trust, and for overseas subscribers should be in pounds sterling drawn on a London Bank.

10 or more copies to one address will qualify for a 10% discount

Back numbers from Spring 1986 available.

Please send to The John Metcalfe Publishing Trust, Church Road, Tylers Green, Penn, Buckinghamshire, HP10 8LN.

All Publications of the Trust are subsidised by the Publishers.

Tract Order Form

Please send to the address below:-

	Price	Quantity
Evangelical Tracts		
The Two Prayers of Elijah	£0.10	......
Wounded For Our Transgressions	£0.10	......
The Blood of Sprinkling	£0.10	......
The Grace of God That Brings Salvation	£0.10	......
The Name of Jesus	£0.10	......
The Death of the Righteous by A.M.S.	£0.10	......
The Ministry of the New Testament	£0.10	......
Repentance	£0.10	......
Legal Deceivers Exposed	£0.10	......
Unconditional Salvation	£0.10	......
Religious Merchandise	£0.10	......
Comfort	£0.10	......
Peace	£0.10	......
Eternal Life	£0.10	......
The Handwriting of Ordinances	£0.10	......
'Lord, Lord!'	£0.10	......

Name and Address (in block capitals)

. . . .

. . . .

. . . .

If money is sent with order please allow for postage. Please address to:- The John Metcalfe Publishing Trust, Church Road, Tylers Green, Penn, Bucks, HP10 8LN.

Tract Order Form

Please send to the address below:-

		Price	Quantity
'Tract for the Times' series			
The Gospel of God	No.1	£0.25	......
The Strait Gate	No.2	£0.25	......
Eternal Sonship and Taylor Brethren	No.3	£0.25	......
Marks of the New Testament Church	No.4	£0.25	......
The Charismatic Delusion	No.5	£0.25	......
Premillennialism exposed	No.6	£0.25	......
Justification and Peace	No.7	£0.25	......
Faith or presumption?	No.8	£0.25	......
The Elect undeceived	No.9	£0.25	......
Justifying Righteousness	No.10	£0.25	......
Righteousness Imputed	No.11	£0.25	......
The Great Deception	No.12	£0.25	......
A Famine in the Land	No.13	£0.25	......
Blood and Water	No.14	£0.25	......
Women Bishops?	No.15	£0.25	......
The Heavenly Vision	No.16	£0.25	......

Name and Address (in block capitals)

. . . .

. . . .

. . . .

If money is sent with order please allow for postage. Please address to:- The John Metcalfe Publishing Trust, Church Road, Tylers Green, Penn, Bucks, HP10 8LN.

Tract Order Form

Please send to the address below:-

		Price	Quantity
Ecclesia Tracts			
The Beginning of the Ecclesia	No.1	£0.10	......
Churches and the Church (J.N.D.)	No.2	£0.10	......
The Ministers of Christ	No.3	£0.10	......
The Inward Witness (G.F.)	No.4	£0.10	......
The Notion of a Clergyman (J.N.D.)	No.5	£0.10	......
The Servant of the Lord (W.H.)	No.6	£0.10	......
One Spirit (W.K.)	No.7	£0.10	......
The Funeral of Arminianism (W.H.)	No.8	£0.10	......
One Body (W.K.)	No.9	£0.10	......
False Churches and True	No.10	£0.10	......
Separation from Evil (J.N.D.)	No.11	£0.10	......
The Remnant (J.B.S.)	No.12	£0.10	......
The Arminian Skeleton (W.H.)	No.13	£0.10	......
Foundation Tracts			
Female Priests?	No.1	£0.25	......
The Bondage of the Will (Martin Luther)	No.2	£0.25	......
Of the Popish Mass (John Calvin)	No.3	£0.25	......
The Adversary	No.4	£0.25	......
The Advance of Popery (J.C. Philpot)	No.5	£0.25	......
Enemies in the Land	No.6	£0.25	......
An Admonition Concerning Relics (John Calvin)	No.7	£0.25	......
John Metcalfe's Testimony against Falsity in Worship	No.8	£0.25	......

Name and Address (in block capitals)

. . . .

. . . .

. . . .

If money is sent with order please allow for postage. Please address to:- The John Metcalfe Publishing Trust, Church Road, Tylers Green, Penn, Bucks, HP10 8LN.